W0006204

37406169R00071

Made in the USA
San Bernardino, CA
17 August 2016

Table of Contents

Preface

Dear Readers,

If your partner/spouse is in the business of sharing and educating others on essential oil, you've come to the right place! I wrote this book specifically to help you support your partner/spouse in building up the business—a successful journey I've made with my own husband since 2011.

I know that some people are hesitant to support this challenging endeavor and may even at times object to or block the business success possibilities. However, this book will give you the tips and techniques you'll both need to succeed. I will share personal development and marriage relationship improvement skills, plus network marketing business activities and events that are instrumental to the success of everyone who is doing this business. I learned all these skills by doing, listening, discussing, and masterminding with top leaders in this business.

Specifically, within these pages, I will

- Teach you a concept on how to identify and honor your social style;
- Urge and help you to discover your own personal major issues and find ways to manage them;
- Remind you of the importance of respecting boundaries;
- Specify and explain the roles I played helping my husband;
- Show you how using your excellent and your genius or unique abilities can maximize the result of your effort;
- Help you identify your WHY in helping your partner/spouse in building up the business; and
- Reveal how to maintain a harmonious partnership or marriage relationship while expanding the business together.

With dedication, cooperation, and hard work, great things are possible!

Liz Wilder

Acknowledgments

This book is definitely the result of a small team who generously shared their valuable time to make this project a reality. I would like to truly thank our enroller, a Blue Diamond, Rachel Harvey Jones, as well as Michele Skousen, Janna Rightmire, Devon Rightmire, and Sunita Pandit for the time they took out from their families and very busy lives to review and peruse the manuscript. You all are so awesome!!!

A sincere appreciation to my other friends and wellness advocates who gave me their thumbs up about the feasibility of this project. That added to my eagerness to finish this book, and to get out of my comfort zone to help thousands of wellness advocates in the MLM business.

My heartfelt gratitude goes to the wellness advocate who conversed with me during the dinner celebration of Diamond-and-above ranks in Utah. She is an angel who whispered good thoughts that stayed in my heart. I wish

I had written down her name. She did not start a joke, but a simple question, and look what I created because of that!

Special thanks to my editor, Renee Nicholls, for her professional editing and proofreading skills, and for the encouragement she gave me.

Most of all, my sincere gratitude to my supportive and dearest husband, Ron for his never-ending nudge to pursue what is in my heart. I appreciate his technology expertise he put into this project. When I felt doubt and fear, Ron reassured me that no matter what happens with this endeavor, things are going to be fine. I know he has my "back" all the time

And last, thanks to you for having the courage to visualize a tremendous future success for you, your spouse or partner, and your family. I want to help you! Make it one of the best decisions you will ever make!

www.crucialpartner.com

Introduction

Recently, one of our wellness advocates told me how happy and grateful she is that her husband is supporting her essential oil business. He motivates and supports her. He does not object to her doing her oil classes, giving oil samples away, or buying supplies and business tools.

On the other hand, I know of a struggling advocate who experiences a great deal of stress every day because even though she is building the essential oil business and taking care of her two children, her husband does not support her. He believes the business is a waste of time, and he will not help her make enough money to compensate for the time he feels that she is taking away from her children and the whole family.

Two years ago, my husband and I attended a business dinner held as a celebration of the

Diamond-and-above ranks. We were sitting with other Diamond and Blue Diamond leaders.

A woman asked me, "So, what do you do in your business?"

I quickly responded, "Oh, I only help my husband. I am always in the background."

Her eyes brightened and opened wider. She instantly replied, "You know, there is no such thing as just helping. You are a big part of that business!"

That was a reality check for me. It was like a clap of thunder that woke me up. It made me realize the truth that my role in our essential oil business really matters. I was very happy about her comment. Now I recognize that what I do to "help" has made a big difference on what we have accomplished in this business.

After that revelation, I thought, "How can I help others like me to feel important, worthy, and proud?

How can I help them recognize that they are actually key players in their partners' network marketing essential oil business? How can I help them make their role of support even stronger?" Finding the answers to these important questions led me to write this book.

The goal of this book is not for spouses or partners to drop what they are currently doing, to abandon their career, or to close their own thriving business. Instead, it is intended to show you the various ways you can continue with your own worthwhile pursuits but also help your partner build the business. Allow yourself to learn what you can do to help your partner succeed. You also can give your support by saying words of encouragement, "Go ahead dear, do what you feel is right," as opposed to asking or telling your partner or spouse to stop immediately in this path of network marketing business.

If you have not become involved, this is a great

time to start supporting your partner's belief in this company and his or her role in the business. Give him or her the nudge of support. Again, stop objecting to what your partner believes about this business. Have faith in the success to come.

I want to amplify the positive results of letting go of your doubts and fear about this network marketing business. If you are hearing negative things from other people, ask questions and seek clarification. Make sure that you and your partner make decisions that are based on valid grounds. Otherwise, if your decisions are influenced by your closed-mindedness, doubts, and fear, then you could be steering you and your partner in the wrong way. You could both be losing opportunities and momentum to be successful in this business!

The truth is, I know a lot of successful couples in this essential oil business. They are reaping the rewards of their success, not only for themselves but for their family as well. These couples are successful because one of them started the business, and the other one decided to give support. Together, they became a powerhouse team!

It does not matter so much what your spouse's rank is now, or what you want to achieve. What matters most is that you recognize that your partner is waiting and wishing that you support her or him in whatever way you can. Not sure how to help? This book is for you!

How This Book Can Help

If you have negative or even lukewarm feelings about your role in all this, I can help you awaken your Purpose or WHY. In Chapter 1, I will enlighten you by showing you various perspectives connected to building the essential oil business with your partner or spouse. Once you realize why it is significant to be on board with your spouse, you'll find that the HOW and WHAT are easy to learn and to implement.

Furthermore, if you follow my approach, you will elevate yourself! Chapter 2 will help you identify your dominant social style. Chapter 3 shows you ways to begin to break the barriers within you. I help you uncover your major personal limiting beliefs and issues so you can begin to find solutions and steps to manage them. This is a genuine personal matter, and it should be taken seriously. Chapter 4, which is about respecting boundaries, can help you decide when to step in and when to hold back. In Chapter 5, I present simple analysis to help you discover your excellent and unique abilities or your genius, and to use those skills to get the outstanding results with the highest use of your valuable time.

It's essential for you to realize you are worthy to be "the" crucial partner in this business. Chapter 6 includes activities, responsibilities, and techniques that can help you be a great team member with your spouse! The vast knowledge you will gain in helping your spouse or partner can stay with you forever. You will be the "wind beneath the wings"!

If you already are supporting your spouse in building the business, congratulations! I aspire for you to continue that path. I hope you pick up a few tips, techniques, clues, and relevant ideas that will enhance your level of expertise. Chapter 7 talks about how you can keep your "boat" sailing on smooth waters.

Last, but surely not the least, I urge you to have your partner or spouse read this book, too. I desire for both of you to understand, highly appreciate, and be grateful for the magnitude of the assistance the supporting spouse or partner contributes to the success of the business.

Let's begin!

Chapter 1

"Why" Do It?

"HE WHO HAS A WHY CAN ENDURE ANY HOW." —FREDERICK NIETZSCHE

"IF YOU FOLLOW YOUR WHY, THEN OTHERS WILL FOLLOW YOU."[1]— SIMON SINEK

People tend to go around in circles giving their reasons on what they do (features) and how they do them (process). They forget the real reasons why they do what they do (belief). Author Simon Sinek explains that when you find your WHY—the core reason why you believe in what you do—the "how" and "what" will follow.

---

[1]Sinek, Simon. Chapter 14, p. 222. *Start With Why*. New York: The Penguin Group (2009).

You Are The Crucial Partner!

Your WHY is actually in you, in your life, in your being. You just need to uncover and identify it, and then believe it one hundred percent. Believe in it without a doubt! In fact, believing in your WHY will attract other believers to join you in your journey.

When you are sure of your WHY, you will find the courage to take the risks necessary to move forward, even when things are tough. It would be very challenging for you to get what you want without your WHY. The truth is, the absence of your WHY could be a cause for your failure.

In 2011, my WHY was to support my spouse in his new opportunity to earn some money. I believed and trusted his vision. I believed this business could bring back our financial freedom, which had dropped in 2008 when his electrical engineering business stopped making money. Three months after he started this business I was involuntarily separated from my corporate job, so I was free to fully support him.

Looking back, I am proud and grateful I was able to help my husband in this business. My WHY evolved, and it is still is evolving. You have to start somewhere. Start with your WHY!

If you have your own business or career where your personal WHY is already set, that is totally fine. As noted, I did not write this book for all spouses and partners to stop their chosen career or close their thriving business. However, our partners or lead spouses still need and deserve our support, even if it's just part-time. Throughout the rest of this chapter, I ask a lot of questions because my goal is to help those who still need to find the WHY that will serve as the heart of that support.

How will you know your own WHY in relation to your spouse or partner's business? Based on my own experience, here are some ways to help you find out.

- First, you have to be *clear* on what you want and why you want it. It all begins with clarity.
- Then, you have to ask yourself what is it that you believe about this business.
- Next, you need to contemplate on your spouse's WHY. Do you believe in your spouse's belief about the company and the opportunities it offers?
- Next, you must contemplate on your family's future. What is it that you believe your family deserves? Why? Where do you want your family to be in the next few years? Why? What experiences do you want your family to have? Why?
- For the next step, you need to look inward. What is it that compels you to act, take risks,

and believe in yourself regardless of any obstacles?

- Finally, you need to ask yourself why you want to join your spouse in the same "boat."

At this point, you may be wondering why it matters for you to know your WHY in helping your spouse. The answer is that your success in helping to build an effective, well-run, profitable business depends highly on your WHY.

CALL TO ACTION:

Write down your possible WHY in helping your partner or spouse in the business.

_____

_____

_____

_____

_____

_____

You Are The Crucial Partner!

_____

_____

_____

_____

_____

_____

_____

_____

_____

Chapter 2

The Four Social Styles

"WILL THE REAL YOU PLEASE STAND UP?"[2]—BOB PHILLIPS

The "Four Social Styles" concept is based on the theory by psychologists David W. Merrill and Roger H. Reid, as discussed in their book-*Personal Styles & Effective Performance.*[3] Each of us has our own communication style and thought process we apply in the behavior we manifest daily. Though we each adopt a part of one or two styles, each of us has a dominant style we identify mostly with, which makes one person unique from another. The role you will play in your business will be dependent on

---

[2] Phillips, Bob. Chapter One, p. 13. *The Delicate Art of Dancing With Porcupines.* California: Regal Books, 1994.

[3] Merrill, David W. and Reid, Roger H. *Personal Styles & Effective Performance. Radnor, PA: Chilton Book Co., 1981.*

the social style of you and your spouse or partner. Do you know your own social style? How about your partner's?

If the business is going to be successful, then it is mandatory to know and accept each other's social styles—why you each act and behave in certain ways. This will lessen the misunderstanding between you. In fact, to achieve lifelong harmony, it is essential to know each other's self-sabotaging, limiting beliefs and personal issues so you can work together to surmount them.

In 2008, my husband and I enrolled in the "Finding Your Soul Purpose" program in Utah. It was a group program conducted by several coaches and speakers. We attended their live events several times for two years. One of the lessons was about finding your own social style.

This program really helped me understand my spouse's social style. For instance, in the past, we had several small to medium-sized, dragged out arguments. It was like a "he said, she said" situation. My approach was, "It's always his fault!" His approach was, "It's always her fault!" (In fact, he always joked he was going to write a book entitled *It is Liz's Fault!*) However, once we recognized these patterns, we were able to calm down and work things out.

I now suggest that couples should learn and understand their social styles, which is the subject for the rest of this chapter. Doing so will improve your relationship with your spouse or partner, with your friends, and with your family members.

The Four Social Styles

1. HEALER OR AMIABLE: Relationship oriented. Not task oriented.

Attributes:

- Is quiet by choice, but witty
- Chooses harmonious relationship, at times, ignoring his or her own feelings

- Has a tendency to heal or solve someone's frustration
- Hates to say "no"; tends to over-commit
- Worries a lot
- Likes to please everyone; follows a "Have a Great Day!" attitude
- Is very sociable and friendly
- Laughs the most but is also the most emotional
- Is patient and notably supportive
- Wants everyone to be happy

Weaknesses:

- Cannot decide quickly or will not make decisions at all
- Is easily distracted, no concrete goals
- Avoids duties and responsibilities
- Is a slow decision maker; acts like the "turtles"
- Avoids closing a sale (says things like, "Tell me your decision later")

How to Deal with Healers:

- Do not expect them to act so soon.

- Seek their help, rather than tell them what to do.

- Let them take their own time.

- Be ready to answer lots of phone calls and texts.

- Provide a whole lot of assurance.

- Allow them to cry, be sentimental, worry, etc.

2. VISIONARY OR EXPRESSIVE: Relationship oriented. "Tell" Assertive.

Attributes:

- Is energetic, like the "chimpanzee"

- Is highly creative—an idea person

- Loves to receive applause and attention

- Is spontaneous and flexible

- Is easily distracted

- Gives you a lot of ideas and possibilities

- Has a great personality; is the life of the party
- Follows the motto "Have a great, fun time!"
- Possesses a high sense of humor
- Enjoys sharing ideas openly with others

Weaknesses:

- Cannot focus on one thing or idea
- Is immensely disorganized
- Shows ADD characteristics
- Does not follow through
- Cannot finish one project
- Is extremely distracted
- Procrastinates
- Doesn't care if time is lost
- Arrives late to most events

How to Deal with Visionaries:

- Remember that anything new is exciting to them.

- Explain things in as short a time as possible.

- Show how much fun things and events will be.

- Say things like, "The party will be a blast!"

- Give them "pep talks."

- Listen to their ideas, visions, and talks

- Allow them to create and envision the flow of events and occasions

3. ORACLE OR ANALYTICAL: Task oriented. "Ask" Assertive.

Attributes

- Is profoundly detail oriented
- Is highly organized
- Is competitive
- Likes to win
- Does research and studies seriously

- Is meticulous and definitive, and appreciates veracity of facts and information
- Has a high standard
- Is a hard worker
- At times, prefers to work alone
- Is sometimes viewed as not a team player
- Asks a lot of questions
- Is not fond of "touchy" feelings
- Could be called the "giraffe"

Weaknesses:

- Prone to view "fun" as unnecessary
- Not so much people oriented but focuses on task results
- Can be self-centered
- At times, wastes time for being too meticulous and very detailed
- Can be annoying with too many questions

- Remembers a lot, and focuses on negatives
- Has the need to be right, which sometimes is a turnoff
- Is occasionally viewed as a slow decision maker, which is a result of the need for definitive information
- Sometimes sets impossible goals

How to Deal with Oracles:

- Give them as much detailed information as possible.
- Be fully patient with their questions and desire for data.
- Respect their desire to be right and need to win.
- Change plans only as needed.
- Let them use their own time at their own pace.
- Leave them alone when you need to.
- Be on exact time, not early or late.

- Change fewer decisions once they've been made.

4. WARRIOR OR DRIVER: Task oriented. "Tell" assertive.

Attributes:

- Get things done with the motto "Just do it!"
- Has a take-charge attitude and moves quickly
- Is confident
- Is hugely goal oriented
- Is a born leader
- Is strong willed
- Is remarkably competitive
- Loves to debate and argue
- Likes to know the bottom line/efficiency
- Is impatient
- Is outspoken, lacks self-control
- Decides quickly
- Is viewed as the "lion"

Weaknesses:

- At times, speaks honestly, which involuntarily hurts others' feelings
- Moves too quickly and forgets some details, which leads to failures
- Can be viewed as pushy
- Hardly relaxes so as to accomplish tasks in as short a time as possible
- Considers expeditious decisions to be normal
- Buys things too quickly
- Focuses on tasks but loses the people connection

How to Deal with Warriors:

- Give them the big pictures of things, not the details.
- Show the bottom line or end results.
- Request permission to explain things.
- Push back, get away, or separate when you feel like it.

- Be prepared to follow or get out of the way.

CALL TO ACTION:

1. Write down your top five strengths and the social style they fall into.

Strengths	Social style

2. Write down your top five weaknesses and the social style they fall into.

Weaknesses	Social style

3. What is your dominant social style?

I think my dominant social style is:

_____

_____

4. Reflection Thoughts: Owning your own social style is outstanding. Be proud of it!

You Are The Crucial Partner!

a. How will my strengths assist my spouse in
building our business?

_____

_____

_____

_____

_____

_____

b. How will my strengths and weaknesses affect my
relationship with our leaders, and business partners?

_____

_____

_____

_____

_____

_____

Chapter 3

Break Your Own Barriers!

"KNOW THYSELF!" *(NOSCE TE IPSUM)*—SOCRATES

"THERE ARE THREE THINGS EXTREMELY HARD: STEEL, A DIAMOND, AND <u>TO KNOW ONE'S SELF</u>." —BENJAMIN FRANKLIN, IN *POOR RICHARD'S ALMANAC*

"THE ONLY CONSTANT IS CHANGE!" —UNKNOWN

As I mentioned in the previous chapter, in order to achieve happiness and success, it is essential for each couple to identify their individual social styles and issues. For me, anger is a major personal issue, and it is part of my limiting beliefs. During my early childhood, my dad abandoned my whole family for ten years. Other experiences during my early adult life also contributed to my state of mind and emotion.

In 2012, my therapist suggested I attend an EMDR session conducted by a licensed psychologist. This approach is based on Eye Movement Desensitization and Reprocessing. It is a psychotherapy treatment that was designed to ease the distress associated with traumatic memories.

I ignored her recommendation for almost half a year. I was ambivalent to admit the truth, but my husband assured me that it would benefit me most to do the therapy. Finally, I attended a few EMDR sessions. I continued my self-work by reading and studying several books about anger. I also attended a lot of personal development programs. I followed the books' self-guided management by journaling and applying the technique exercises when needed. Yes, I now know myself!

You must do whatever it takes to know and fix your major personal issues affecting your life and your relationships. The knowledge you will learn about yourself will help you to apply proper behavior in different circumstances. There will be less frustration, and "burning of bridges" with your relationships. You will manage your emotions better, and you will reap positive results in life and in business.

Hiring a professional therapist to help you identify and accept your barriers is the first step. The rest of the solution process is up to you! It will be challenging but worth it. You will be glad when you did this. I know I am!

Here is a sample of major personal issues:

- Jealousy

- Anger

- Fear, of all sorts

- Sex addiction

- Drug addiction

- Alcoholism

- Control issues

- Pathological lying

- Narcissism

- Abuse, all types

- Feelings of shame

- Depression

- Guilt feelings

No therapist can solve 100 percent of your major personal issues. The bulk of work depends on you!

- Seek the professional help of a therapist who can assist you to overcome your major personal issues.

- Hire a life coach you can afford—one who can be objective, honest, and whom you can trust.

- Find a mentor who will lift you up no matter what—that is, who believes in your greatness even at your worst time. Friends and relatives can great be mentors.

- Read books, do research, do journaling, and join a support group to help you in this undertaking.

- Practice! Put to action the solutions and apply appropriate techniques.

Most of all, celebrate the *improved you*, no matter what!

CALL TO ACTION:

Write down the major personal issues that you believe are affecting your personal and business relationships. (Use another piece of paper if you need more space.)

_____

_____

_____

_____

Chapter 4

Respecting Boundaries

"BOUNDARIES IN MARRIAGE, IS NOT ABOUT FIXING, CHANGING, OR PUNISHING YOUR MATE."[4]—HENRY CLOUD AND JOHN TOWNSEND

"BOUNDARIES...IS NOT MEANT TO CONTROL BUT RATHER TO BE RESPONSIBLE..."—SERENA WANG

When my husband decided to pursue this career, he first signed up as an Independent Product Consultant, (now called a Wellness Advocate). It was clear that he would be the lead spouse to build our business. From the beginning, he studied the company history and the compensation plan. He analyzed the products and the placement strategies.

---

[4] Cloud, Henry and Townsend, John. p.11. *Boundaries In Marriage*. Michigan: Zondervan, 2002.

I have always believed that my husband cracked the code on the compensation plan. He studied it. He knows it will work. He believes it is a better compensation plan than other MLM (multi-level marketing) he has been involved with before.

My social style is a Warrior, while my husband is an Oracle. One of the reasons why we have disagreements is because our social styles are opposite each other. I can make a quick decision without too much information, while he needs to analyze all the information before he makes a decision. Respecting boundaries is the key to our successful discourse on matters of our relationship and in business.

In fact, respecting boundaries shows courtesy and it emphasizes consideration for the other person's feelings. It allows you to master positive virtues, and it prepares you to be a very effective wellness advocate. More importantly, your marriage will retain harmony.

There can be only one major leader in a relationship, be it in marriage or business partnership. In short, I realized early on that my husband is the "lead," and I am the "support." Being aware of our own roles made it clear where and how to respect boundaries between us.

It is of the utmost necessity to acknowledge the boundaries between you and your spouse. There will be times when—in your desire to help and solve the issues at hand—you will tend to rush into giving your solution immediately. Wait! Your spouse or partner needs to give her or his point of view or ideas on the solution. Then you both can analyze the best solution. Your suggestion may be the best in your mind, but your partner's suggested solution could be valid too.

Ultimately, it is a matter of coming to the meeting of the minds—that is, which one is a better solution, and who should acquiesce. It does not matter what your rank is now, or what you are striving to achieve. It is imperative that you both recognize what role each of you wishes to perform.

My husband and I have had to work hard on this principle. Although we discuss the solution beforehand, most of the time his solution is most appropriate to the circumstance. Since I know I am the "support" spouse and he is the "lead" in this business, his ideas and solutions come first.

As the support spouse you can:

- Promote and accept your spouse's ideas.
- Listens to his or her advice.
- Follow through and help implement his or her vision for the business.
- Accept the knowledge and experiences he or she wants to share with you.
- Acknowledge the boundaries he or she requested between the two of you.

As the lead spouse you can:

- Appreciate your spouse's enthusiasm and increased confidence.

- Show gratefulness in her or his effort.

- Develop a shared vision.

- Promote his or her achievements.

- Supports her or his business dreams and current events.

- Give or allow her or him more duties if requested or warranted.

CALL TO ACTION

1. Write down three instances where you respected your partner's boundary.

_____

_____

_____

_____

_____

2. Make it a habit to write this accomplishment in your journal. Keep a separate journal to record your personal journey, as you become a crucial partner in this business. Start your journal here.

_____

_____

_____

_____

_____

_____

_____

Chapter 5

Manifest Your Genius or Unique Ability®[5]

"AKIN TO THE MOVIE THE GOOD, THE BAD AND THE UGLY, WHICH ONE WOULD YOU CHOOSE?" —LIZ WILDER

The highest and best use of your time, talents, resources, and skills is a valuable contribution to your business. Do you want to maximize your contributions? Then you have to know your incompetence, competence, excellent skills, and unique ability skills. High awareness of these weaknesses and skills will save you energy and

---

5   Trademark of The Strategic Coach, Inc. / Dan Sullivan.

reduce your frustration. It is paramount for you to know your unique ability or your genius—the ability or genius that gets you what you want and gives you high satisfaction and success!

I know this topic is vast, as I have gone through the full process myself. Discovering my unique abilities was an important realization for me, and I desire the same for each of you. The process of discovering your unique abilities or genius requires your commitment to step out of your comfort zone, do a lot of discovery exercises, and learn to accept what is working and what is not. In this chapter, we will consider the principles behind this concept.

Incompetent Skills

Do you usually do daily activities out of necessity, but you do not get satisfaction? If so, this makes you feel unproductive and unhappy. You feel you wasted your valuable time. This is *Incompetent Skill.* We all have incompetent skills we use where we usually become easily frustrated. Most often, the results are useless: wrong outcome; lots of mistakes; frustration and stress; conflict with others; and high dissatisfaction. That is because you do not have the complete knowledge and appropriate skills to do the tasks effectively.

For example, let's say you do your own taxes when you do not know all the rules and procedures of doing it. Or, you do your own bookkeeping and accounting when you are not trained in those skills.

Stop doing things and activities you are 100 percent unqualified to do. You are wasting your valuable time!

Competent Skills

This is the area in your life where—no matter how much you try to do the activities—you feel your performance is only an average: you do repetitive tasks; you easily get bored; and you feel you will fail. Most of the time, you never come out ahead of the others. That is because you have to compete with others who have the best skills, training, and high aptitude. In other words, they are more competent in what they do than you are! The reality is, you are not inspired to get better. Your feeling is, "Do not disrupt the status quo. Leave it the way it is!" But when you get stuck in this pattern, you may simply be wasting your time.

I used to run 5K and 10K races in my thirties and early forties. Each time I wanted to place first in my age category, but I did not. I only reached the finish line almost out of breath! I did not have the physical endurance and mental aptitude in running. I knew I did only a mediocre training. When you find yourself in a similar situation, remember that it is ok to compete, but that is not always the best way to prove your worth in life. There are other ways to prove your worth to yourself and to others. I finally allowed myself to drop it, and I was content.

Another example would be someone who feels maintaining and cutting the grass is not the best use of his or her time. That person is competent in cutting the grass and knows perfectly well how to operate the lawn mower. It only takes about one hour a week to do it, but the person isn't happy and feels bored doing it. Some options would be to hire a neighborhood kid to do it, to use the time to listen to fun music on headphones, or even to replace the lawn with a patio that doesn't need to be mowed. The point is, if something isn't working well for you, don't feel compelled to keep doing that exact same thing in the exact same way. Find a way to drop it altogether, get someone else to do it for you, or make some better choices!

Excellent Skills

Excellent skills are important. You are productive when you use your excellent skills. People admire you for those skills because you have a high standard in performing them. You have success in projects where you apply your excellent skills. The results are always great! But—and it's a big but—no matter what your successes are, you would not choose to do more of these activities. "No passion" is a short phrase to describe excellent skills. At times, you feel trapped because they take so much of your valuable time. There is no more time left to do the "really cool and fun stuff"!

It is all right for people to do things they excel at, especially when they get paid for doing them. A good example is an employee who sticks to a job because it pays the family's bills and needs. Employees like this become excellent at what they do because of repetitive, routine, daily tasks. That happens for millions of people, and it is ok. Sometimes the need to put food on the table and a roof over your head is a priority. Just remember: There is always a price for what you choose to do. At some point, you will feel some success doing these things, but in the end you will not have a major feeling of accomplishment.

In my case, cooking is a great example. I like to cook hot meals. I am excellent in following recipes. At times, I even create recipes from scratch. My husband and my friends like the meals I prepare. However, even though I enjoy cooking, I've never wanted to go to cooking school to become a chef. I do not have the passion to become a professional chef. To achieve the highest sense of accomplishment, we must move beyond our comfort zone of excellent skills and identify and then pursue our unique skills and abilities.

Your Genius, or Unique Ability® [6]

Unique Ability concept is created by Dan Sullivan and Babs Smith, founders of the Strategic Coach® [7]

---

[6] Registered Trademark - Strategic Coach Program/Dan Sullivan.

[7] Trademark of The Strategic Coach, Inc.

Program. Have you ever heard someone say, "I love what I do! I would do it for free!"? This is where your *passion* comes into play. Unique ability is doing an activity with less perceived effort. It happens so naturally because you have the talent to do it! You use your innate "genius" in this activity; this can also be called your "Aha" breakthrough moment. Dan Sullivan calls this your "Unique Ability." With proper training, you can easily improve and become expert in it. You can do this activity day in and day out—and you would want to do it even if you didn't get paid.

My husband started fixing radios and televisions during his high school days. He fixed broken Porsche car radios for a Porsche dealership in Marin County, California. He helped many classmates and teachers fix their televisions and radios, and he made a lot of friends doing this. One time, a motorcycle group of students defended him against a bully student who challenged him to fight "mano a mano." He loves electronics, but not fighting! He graduated as an electrical engineer from U.C. Berkeley. Lately, he fixed our large, flat-screen television, which involved replacing lots of capacitors and some "chips." Voila! The TV looks brand new! I tell people he could fix anything that connects to electricity. This is one of his geniuses or unique abilities where he has passion.

It is ideal to spend more time practicing your unique ability or using your genius. Do things you have a passion for. Nourish and grow your strengths.

The Essential Oil Business and Your Excellent and Unique Abilities

Now that you are aware of your incompetence (the "ugly"), the competence (the not so "bad"), the excellent (the "good"), and your unique abilities or your "genius" (the "aha" moment), let us relate that to your essential oil business.

Discovering your excellent and unique abilities is a serious undertaking. It is worth the time and financial investment you will make. Here are some questions to consider:

- What are the skills and abilities you have passion for that you can contribute to the success of your essential oil business?
- What roles can you take on that will cultivate the highest and best use of your time and abilities?
- What are you willing to do to be more productive, be more creative, create less tension, and foster harmony in your business?
- Most of all, what is it you do with passion?

When Do You Hire Professional Help?

During the early stages of our business, we did everything to save money because we couldn't afford to do otherwise. We decided to invest in the business to grow it. There will come a stage in your business when you will be able to pay someone else to do certain tasks. This is true: "If it is not your genius, let someone with genius and passion for them, do those things!" You and your spouse or partner both have to decide which tasks can best be accomplished by hiring outside professional help.

Professional Help Is a Good Decision When . . .

- You both are incompetent in doing certain tasks.

- You both are competent in doing the tasks, but the results are substandard, and you both are unhappy about them.

- The business is successful enough, and you are both busy doing moneymaking activities.

- The business is making so much money that, for both of you, your time is more valuable when it's spent doing activities to expand your business (e.g., conducting training, retreats, and workshops for your wellness advocates).

- It is more important to spend time with family (e.g., attending your child's piano or dance recital, or a wedding of a friend or a close family member).

Some Professional Helpers:

- Babysitter or caregiver
- Housecleaner
- Cook or chef for meal preparations and meal planning
- Maid to do laundry, clothes ironing, and other errands
- Caterer, for meal needs for big groups during training or retreats
- Bookkeeper
- Accountant

- Tax preparer

- Travel agent

- Gardener

- Event planner (for your training)

- Life and business coach

- Home improvement carpenter, painter, designer, electrician

- Automobile mechanic

- Personal assistant

- Administrative assistant

- Editor or proofreader

CALL TO ACTION:

Write down in the following worksheets the common activities you do. Can you identify what your incompetent, competent, excellent, and unique abilities are? What can you do to highlight your unique ability skills and practice them in your essential oil business?

Incompetent Skills

Activities/Tasks	How you felt on the outcome

Competent Skills

Activities/Tasks	How you felt on the outcome

Excellent Skills

Activities/Tasks	How you felt on the outcome

Your Genius or Unique Abilities

Activities/Tasks	How you felt on the outcome

Chapter 6

Supporting Roles

"WE ALL CARRY A RESPONSIBILITY TO DO WHAT WE CAN WHEN IT WILL MAKE A DIFFERENCE." –MICHAEL USEEM

In 2008, in our quest to reinvent ourselves, we went on a journey to learn many new things. We studied internet marketing, network marketing, how to find your soul purpose, and how to become authors and public speakers. We became lifetime members of CEO Space International, which offers business growth conferences *(http://ceospaceinternational.com/)*. We attended several live and online events of other coaching programs based in Utah. We paid business and life coaches. I joined a few speaking coaching programs to improve myself. My first collaborative book was published in the fall of 2009. Then in June of 2011, my husband was introduced to the network marketing business of essential oils. In August of 2011, my employment with the federal judiciary system was severed. That was when I assisted my husband in this business full-time. I decided that, for the moment, I would put aside my desire to become a public speaker to empower women.

In the beginning, what was important to me was to comprehend everything about essential oils. I read the complete book about essential oils, and I studied one essential oil every night. I did not waste time. I watched educational webinars and participated in essential oil prospecting events. I learned to conduct essential oil classes by myself. Later on, I immersed myself in related business and personal development programs. In fact, I have attended leadership retreats and annual conventions for five years now. Today I assist in conducting business training and workshops, and other business-building activities.

The degree of your desire to help your spouse plays an immense part in what you can contribute to the success of your business. With tenacious desire, you can learn any skill. My background is in the legal field, social work, and administration. I did not have any knowledge of essential oils, or knowledge in the concept of alternative healing. But that did not stop me from studying as much as I needed to equip myself about network marketing and essential oils. I have come out of my comfort zone to learn many facets of this business. I even passed the online course on Chemistry of Essential Oil, which was my first exposure to organic chemistry! I am a certified instructor in the specialized essential oil application technique since July of 2012.

As you can see, I ventured into some unknown endeavors to increase my comprehension of this industry. That is how I approached this business to become my husband's crucial business partner. I hope you will, too!

Even though my husband was the key player, and he was both knowledgeable and familiar with the approaches I've just described and the ones that appear in the list below, I took it upon myself to learn them too. I also encourage you to learn and execute most of them—although, of course, you may choose only those you would like to learn and those that correspond to your excellent and unique skills, along with your type of personality.

The following activities, roles, and pursuits are listed in no exact particular order. **<u>Please remember, these are only suggestions for you to consider.</u>** Knowing them does not guarantee your own success as the crucial partner. Instead, you have to put them into action. Action creates certainty. Certainty creates success!

1. Study Your Company and Learn About Its Products

- Learn the company history and background of the owners/founders.

- Check out the company mission and goals.

- Learn network marketing or direct selling business principles.

- Study and learn all you can about the essential oils and the related products.

- Watch and listen to live and recorded webinars.

- Join in the team calls about pertinent courses to increase your confidence in the business.

- Use the essential oils and the related products to maximize your experiences with them.

2. Understand Your Business Account

- Learn how to navigate in your account using an online back office system.

- Learn how to create and modify monthly product order and use the different processing methods.

- Learn how to understand statistics parameters (e.g., the graphic tree and the monthly performance report).

- Learn how to understand the commission reports.

- Learn how to use e-blast email system to communicate with your advocates.

- Learn how to enroll new wellness advocates or distributors using your back office or smart phone App.

- Learn how to understand your business account (e.g., increase in your overall volume and the total number of distributors in your organization).

- Understand the monthly promotions and how to promote them.

- Use your back office to learn the latest information on other events, tools, and get quick reports.

3. Prospect for Your Business

- Participate in fairs and events.
- Set up booth/table with products display in paid or free events.
- Attend networking events.
- Meet and share these oils with people you do not know who come to your table or display.
- Raffle a product using their business cards or have them complete a small card to include in the raffle.
- Gather information from people who talked to you during the fairs and events (e.g., name, email address, and cell phone number).

- Make calls and send follow up emails on new prospects you met and connected with.
- Share with a lot of people all the benefits you and your partner or spouse has experienced.
- Build friendships with new people you meet. Show your interest in them, their family, and their health issues.

4. Share Essential Oils and Other Products with Everyone

- Bring products to share with relatives, friends, neighbors, coworkers, and others.
- Invite them to your house for an oil party or any appropriate occasion.
- Go to their house to show and share the products.
- Use social media to pique interest (e.g., Facebook, Instagram, Pinterest). Tell people

the information is there, and remember to be FDA compliant in your language usage.

5. Educate and Enroll Prospects

- Conduct essential oil classes.

- Schedule dates of classes.

- Invite new prospects to your essential oil classes.

- Make phone calls, send texts, and send emails as a follow-up for class attendance confirmation.

- Teach different types of essential oil classes that suit your prospects like mothers, teachers, active people, couples, etc.

- Prepare and study for the class.

- Display the essential oil bottles and other products on a table.

- Give enough oil experiences to all attendees.

- Give wild orange and peppermint "wow" experience.

6. Conduct One-On-One Presentations

- Remember that one-on-one presentation is the more personal approach to educating your prospects to get at least one hour of your personal attention and education.

- Offer one-on-one presentations to those prospects that could not make it to a regular essential oil class.

- Give prospects personalized answers to inquiries made during the one-on-one presentation.

7. Sign Up New Distributors/Wellness Advocates

- Use the paper form to obtain the mandatory information for you to be able to sign up the new wellness advocate.

- Sign up wellness advocates using your back office online signing/registration system.

- Show new distributors how to use the back office system (e.g., how to set up monthly order templates; how to redeem free points, etc.).

- Show them how to use the oils and products.

- Give them their new distributor or wellness advocate numbers, which they should keep in their possession, input on their cell phone, or write on a piece of paper and leave in their wallet or purse.

- Give them the Customer Service Department telephone number.

8. Attend Company Events

Leadership Retreats (For qualified ranks)

- Organize a team lunch in a restaurant.

- Invite all your team members attending.

- Procure an affordable hotel accommodation close to the event location.

- To save advocates some money organize hotel room sharing arrangements.

Three-Day Annual Convention

- Be the first to hear and to learn of the new product launches
- Learn the continued growth of the company from the founders themselves.
- Attend the formal Gala, a formal dinner celebration and a "red carpet" walk of new Diamonds-and-above ranks.
- Meet and network with the owners of the company.
- Meet other high-ranking distributors or wellness advocates (i.e., Blue Diamonds and Presidential Diamonds).
- Attend business and personal development seminars conducted by Diamond-and-above ranks Leaders.

- Celebrate with the members of your organization and team up-lines (i.e., dinner and party).

The Annual Incentive Trip

- Fulfill requirements set up by the company to win a free annual incentive trip or annual vacation for distributors or wellness advocates.
- If you did not qualify for a free trip, consider "buying in" to join.

9. Get Certified

- Attend related certification courses.
- Become certified to practice essential oil application techniques.
- Become certified as instructor to teach essential oil application techniques (Need to fulfill rank qualification).

- Consider taking an online course and getting certified in the chemistry of essential oils. (Voluntary basis not mandatory)

10. Conduct Essential Oil Application Technique Certification Classes

- Update the class calendar on your website (if you have one).

- Create the PayPal or Ticket Leap button for student registration and online payment.

- Order supplies for the class (e.g., oil kits, oil belts, etc.).

- Announce via e-blast email system and posts on social media (e.g., Facebook group).

- Prepare and study for the class.

- Gather the paraphernalia and display on the table for student registration.

- Make sure all the students are on the list of attendees.

- Register each student and give them oils, brochures, and other miscellaneous paraphernalia.

- Give one-hour PowerPoint presentation about the essential oil application technique.

- Assist in the hands-on training of each student during the class.

- Assist in teaching other related techniques: Hands-on technique, etc.

- Consider traveling to other cities to conduct this class. This can be beneficial if there are enough registered students to cover for the costs of supplies, travel, and time and effort spent.

11. Up-Level Your Personal and Business Development Skills

- Learn various personal improvement and business-building techniques.

- Gain more leadership skills.

- Learn and practice relationship building.

- Listen to weekly group calls on various topics.

- Attend seminars and workshops on business development (e.g., how to follow-up, how to close a sale, how to approach different types of people, etc.). Nowadays, you can find most of these trainings on YouTube and other online sites sponsored by other high-rank business leaders.

- Know your own personality type and social styles.

- If you can afford, hire a life and business coach to help you manage your personal major issues and self-sabotaging limiting beliefs.

- Find a mentor you can trust.

12. Assist in the Rank Advancement

- Assist in the decision-making process with your spouse to advance rank.

- Monitor your organization and the monthly overall volume.
- Prepare a list of products to buy, if necessary (i.e., the name of oil and corresponding product value or PV).
- At the end of each month, stay up late to make sure all the necessary product orders are in the system.

13. When Qualified, Join the Diamond Club Challenge

- Learn more about Diamond Club, a program open in the summer and fall that is sponsored by the company and your Diamond, Blue Diamond, and Presidential Diamond leaders to help wellness advocates (Premier, Silver, and Gold) advance to a higher rank. (We did the challenge in summer of 2012. The experiences, knowledge, and friendships we gained were worth all the work we did!)

- Note that the monthly product promotions and incentives during this program help in gaining enrollment.

- As a participant, be sure to travel to certain cities and states where you have business leaders to conduct essential oil classes.

- Conduct the required number of essential oil classes in your own city also.

- Watch your overall volume grow and advance your rank while you help your leaders and other advocates to advance rank too.

- Participate in the award ceremony to recognize participants with their achievements.

14. Participate in Rank Advancement Training

- Take part in the Elites-and-above Retreats sponsored by your Diamond, Blue Diamond, and Presidential Diamond leaders.

- Join in the Diamond-and-above rank mastermind events in your group.

- Take advantage of the many online rank advancement programs and books offered by many Diamond, Blue Diamond, and Presidential Diamond leaders.

15. Oversee the Clerical Administration of the Business

Finances and Bookkeeping

- Pay household and other business expenses online or by mailing checks to vendors.

- Drive to the bank location and deposit checks to the bank.

- Alternately, learn to deposit to your bank via an online system or using your bank's app.

- Update your check registry book.

- When necessary, lend personal financial assistance to your own business.

Product Inventory

- Maintain inventory of all your essential oils and products. This helps to keep track of what you have and what you need to buy for the current month's order.

- Maintain a "Borrow & Return" binder to keep track of borrowed items by your wellness advocates. Sometimes, wellness advocates borrow oil and products either for classes or event display use. Don't trust your memory—write it down!

- Make sure any oils and other products borrowed are returned and/or paid for. Follow the agreement between you, your

spouse or partner, and the borrowing
wellness advocate.

- If you prefer, create this tracking system
  using your computer.

Filing System

- Create and maintain a simple filing system
  (e.g., receipts, brochures, and pamphlets).

- Refer to your filing system during the tax
  season. Filing receipts of all purchases you
  made is a good business practice.

- Label each folder properly, which makes it
  easy to locate the files when you need them.

16. Participate in Social Media

- Post comments, events, promotions, wins,
  pictures, and respond to relevant topics on
  Facebook (FB) through your own team FB
  page; a direct up line FB page; a Diamond-
  and-above ranks FB page; the company
  Diamond-and-above FB page; and the

Diamond-and-above essential oil application technique Q&A FB page.

- Use other sites such as Instagram and Pinterest to reach out and promote your business.

17. Assist Leaders and Down Lines

- Create, build, and maintain an appropriate business relationship with your leaders and down lines (e.g., know their family, join them in their events).
- If requested, conduct classes on their behalf.
- Take part in your leaders' activities/events (e.g., DIY class and summer appreciation events).
- Secure contract for cheaper hotel rooms for annual leadership retreat.
- Lend some financial support, if necessary (this is optional but not required).

- Lend essential oils or other products for display, demonstration, or to share in their classes.

- Once a month during the monthly business training, give a motivational or an inspirational talk.

- Join in the weekly team call by teaching for one hour about a product or give a motivational pep talk.

- Communicate with distributors or wellness advocates via phones, texting, email, and FB chat about products, leadership retreats, conventions, and personal challenges.

- Answer inquiries on our essential oil application technique certification classes.

- Applaud, suggest, and show approval on their accomplishments during a business enrollment challenge.

- Announce their name and rank during your monthly training. Ask them to share something related to their "wins."
- Post their names and rank advancement on all FB groups related to your business.

- Cook at your home, or organize a potluck dinner or sit down dinner at your own home for a few wellness advocates.
- Do once-a-year Christmas potluck dinner for all local wellness advocates, either at your home or at the desired location.
- Join in with other leaders in their group Christmas party.
- Join other leaders at a Lunch or Dinner Treat As Rank Advancement Celebration.
- Invite each of your new Silver-and-above ranks leaders and their spouse to a meal.
- Give bottles of essential oil or other items as gifts.

18. Help Your Leaders in Their Classes

- Act as a host or hostess and prepare snacks or drinks.

- Make sure the training room is tidy and that chairs and display tables are clean.

- Participate in the discussion when necessary.

- When requested, assist in the class presentation.

- Assist in closing and enrolling new wellness advocates, when needed.

19. Act as Supply Officer to Your Leaders and Down Lines

- Whenever possible, we took advantage of free shipping offered by several suppliers, or bought the essential oil books and vital supplies in bulk to help our new distributors, (e.g., oil belt, oil bags, oil labels, and oil vials).

- Sell these essential oil books at bulk price to distributors for them to use as incentive to their new sign-ups.

- On occasion, sell these books and supplies in bulk price to your local monthly business training events.

- Maintain an inventory list of supplies.

- Collect and deposit funds into the proper business bank account.

20. Assist to Run Monthly Business Trainings

Outside Venues

- Locate feasible business training venues.

- Assist in securing and signing the venue contract.

- Attend your training and classes.

- Make sure the venue is set up completely:
    1) Proper number of chairs is set up;

2) Table(s) for registration of attendees is in place;

3) Appropriate big screen is set up;

4) A podium or small elevated stage is arranged;

5) Microphone is on hand and working;

6) Water service, if included in the contract, is provided;

7) Small table for laptop or computer is available;

8) Other paraphernalia is on hand as needed.

- Arrive at least ninety minutes early to the event location.

- Gather and bring necessary paraphernalia to the event:

  a. Display banner(s);

  b. Attendees' name list; raffle tickets; raffle prizes; diffuser; raffle oils; pens; and writing paper.

c. Miscellaneous items:

- Table cloths
- Portable screen
- Microphone
- Portable small 3x3 feet table
- Laptop

In-Home Training/Classes

- Make sure all chairs needed are in place.
- Prepare some drinks or snacks.
- Prepare sign-up forms.
- Do raffle of oil and products.
- Choose and make oils and other products ready for giveaway.
- Make sure diffusers are turned on diffusing essential oil while class is taking place.

21. Serve as a Speaker or as a Trainer

- Choose and study relevant topics.

- Give a motivational speech when appropriate.

- Read books, and do research on your chosen topic.

- Create and prepare the lesson in PowerPoint format.

- Give a "Call to Action" lesson at the end of the event.

- Print any related materials of your chosen topic for distribution during the class.

22. Participate in Nonprofit Activities

- Participate in the company's nonprofit activities assisting underprivileged people around the world.

- Take part in the "acts of giving back" to communities where you go for the annual incentive trip (e.g., giving school supplies, renovating schools, and building water supply systems).

- Donate monthly to the company's nonprofit entity.

- Volunteer to join in the humanitarian trip to underprivileged countries around the world.

23. Organize Activities to Relieve Your Spouse or Partner of Other Daily Duties

- Assume more duties to care for your children and/or parents (e.g., driving them to school, games, and doctor's appointments).

- If you have babies or very young children, assume more responsibilities to take care of them.

- If you have pets, assume more pet care responsibility.

- Act as a travel agency for you both. Finding cheaper flights and hotels online can save you both time and frustration. Also, finding affordable ways to vacation online can be rewarding too.

CALL TO ACTION:

1. Write down a few activities from the list above where you can use your excellent and unique abilities:

_____

_____

_____

_____

_____

_____

_____

_____

_____

Chapter 7

Smooth Sailing of Your "Boat"

"LIKE ALL VOYAGES, IMPROVING YOUR MARRIAGE BEGINS BY SUSPENDING DISBELIEF, TAKING ONE SMALL STEP...SEEING WHERE YOU ARE AND TAKING THE NEXT STEP."[8] – JOHN M. GOTTMAN

Building a network marketing business is quite similar to building any other business. The differences lie in the approach, systems, and protocols. As you've learned throughout this book, foremost is preserving the harmonious relationship between you and your partner or spouse. In this chapter, I will discuss a few principles that I feel are

---

[8] Gottman, John M., Afterword, p. 277. *The Seven Principles for Making Marriage Work.* New York: Harmony Books, 2015.

necessary to maintain a harmonious personal relationship while doing the business together.

Trust and Faith

Trust and faith are interchangeable in a few ways. They rely on the integrity, strength, ability, and surety of a person or thing. The trust and faith you give to your spouse in the business venture you both are in matter so much!

Initially, I had doubts about my husband's decision to launch his network marketing essential oil business. I knew some people had offered him engineering projects. Some were quite big and challenging projects. Once I actually told him, "You can make more money being an engineer than doing that network marketing."

However, when he insisted that this business would be great and is very doable, I felt he believed in the company and its products. I then had faith that he would succeed in this business. My two grown children are independent, and we did not have other family issues as distractions. From then on, I trusted his vision. I am glad I did!

Self-Respect, Pride, and Respect Toward Your Spouse

Self-respect and feeling proud are paramount. It is critical that you are feeling proud that you are assisting your partner or spouse to the fullest of your capability. Being on board with your partner or spouse in the business is admirable.

Second, it is endearing to treat your partner or spouse with high courtesy and consideration. Remember, this is the person with whom you share your life and business. It shows respect when you say, "Okay, dear, I will help you in this network marketing business. Tell me how best I can help you." Wellness advocates respect your partner or spouse for helping them build their own businesses. He or she deserves your respect as well.

Enthusiasm, Caring, and High Sense of Responsibility

In August of 2011, I was involuntarily separated from my corporate job. My husband said, "Liz, I'd like you to help me build this business," and I listened to him. I quickly embraced enthusiasm and excitement. I immediately decided to be on this "boat," and I helped him in building this business. I supported him! As I mentioned in earlier chapters, I was enthused to read any books about essential oils. I listened and participated in many "live" and recorded seminars, webinars, and group calls. I cared, and I was responsible enough to take on many duties.

Before you read further, take a moment to review the content of this book and consider how you could show your enthusiasm, care, and a high sense of responsibility as an excellent partner in your essential oil business.

Smooth Sailing of Your "Boat"

Acceptance, Validation, Understanding, and Forgiveness (Taking the High Road)

As I've mentioned, my husband and I have the almost exact opposite of social styles, although we did have some similar childhood experiences. The important thing is that we've both done a lot of work to ensure our personal healing and growth, and I strongly encourage you to do the same.

You know those PTSDs from childhood? They will haunt and follow you in your adult life unless you take the time to heal them. In our case, we both have done a lot of self-work to understand and to forgive each other's shortcomings. This requires self-awareness, acceptance, and a full understanding of our own self-sabotaging, limiting beliefs. There are still times when we are tempted to let our limiting beliefs rule our lives, but we work hard to overcome this. It is hard, but constant self-reminders help a lot.

Learn to accept, validate, and understand all about your partner's, or spouse's negative childhood background. Holding on to grudges does not have any positive effect at all. No one is perfect. We are all not perfect. Celebrate his or her positive traits! Taking the high road all the time is outstanding!

How did we do it? We hired life and business coaches. At first, it was not easy to face the truths. But it pays off when you do. We learned to accept, validate, understand, and forgive each other.

Before you move on, consider what you would do to know both yourself and your spouse. What would you do to become an effective team?

Apology and Accountability

As the Canadian cartoonist Lynn Johnston notes, "An apology is the Superglue of life. It can repair just about anything!" According to the *Merriam-Webster Dictionary*, an apology is "a statement saying that you are sorry about something : an expression of regret for having done or said something wrong" (*www.merriam-webster.com/dictionary/apology*).

Your primary goal in showing an apology is to ease someone's emotional burden and garner forgiveness. The vital issue of who should be the focus of the apology is the reason why so many apologies seem phony. It is not just about making yourself free of guilt for what has transpired. Your concern is to make your partner or spouse feel better, although your own feelings of guilt or regret will be comforted when you know you have apologized.

Your apology means several things. It may mean admitting your mistake, a mishap, a wrong decision, and inappropriate behavior. It shows you value your relationship with your partner or spouse more than your ego. It repairs ruptures in your relationship. It proves your accountability and responsibility for the impact of your actions and behavior. Here are some suggestions to give an effective apology and request forgiveness.

- Say with honesty the "I'm sorry statement."

- Point out your regret for what happened.

- Acknowledge that you violated your spouse's feelings.

- Give an empathy statement to recognize the impact of your actions toward your spouse.

Keeping Up the Love for Each Other

When our first marriage therapist heard our story, he said that it is a lovely story. Indeed, it is! Our first challenge was to take turns every weekend to travel 350 miles each way to visit each other for a year and a half. Part of our story is somewhat akin to the movie *Planes, Trains, and Automobiles.* We alternately took every other weekend to visit each other, and his parents. We drove. I flew via commercial plane. He flew his private small plane to my town. We rode the Greyhound bus. We took the Amtrak train. All this effort to be with each other! That—and all the other realities we weathered—led to our wedding day.

"Always come from your heart," is a concept that uses the heart's reasons. It means using your intuition in solving most issues. When you choose to validate and understand, that is coming from the heart. When you choose to let go of your ego and your high pride that, is coming from the heart. When you choose to love, to forgive, and apply humility, that is coming from the heart. When you choose to be in harmony with your spouse or partner, instead of insisting on being right, that is coming from the heart. When you apply the courage to accept you are wrong, that is coming from the heart. When you apply compassion and empathy, you are coming from the heart. Remembering this concept will help to keep the love between you and your spouse.

Whenever an issue comes up that I know is

solvable, I try not to react subjectively. I am not saying I am now an expert on this, but it has helped me to respond to the current situation objectively. To respond with reasons from the heart rather than reacting with negative emotion works well. My husband is using this "come from your heart" concept also.

You and your spouse or partner likely have limiting beliefs that—most of the time—negatively affect the outcome of the issue. The "Come from your heart, not from your mind" concept works! As I mentioned earlier, most of the time, the concept of the mind's insistence ("I am right, and you are wrong") does not work.

Truly loving someone requires the application of hundreds of relationship techniques and principles. But one thing is true: Keep an open communication, and most things will smoothly follow. I always believe that when love is present, other things come easy.

Being Grateful for Your Spouse's Vision

Why be grateful? First, it makes you happier and content in your life. When you are grateful for all the small and big things you have now, you feel content. You surrender to the other unwanted events in your life. Be aware of ALL your blessings, and be grateful for them every day.

Are you grateful for the opportunity to become a *crucial partner* in the success of your business? Will it be an easy or a hard decision for you to make to join your partner or spouse in the business? I know you are grateful for your partner or spouse and everything he or she does for you and your family. Are you grateful for his or her vision to be successful in this business? That attitude of gratitude makes you a humble human being.

I am grateful my husband joined this business as early as he did. I am grateful he asked me to help him build this business. For the most part, it was an easy decision for me. I am grateful he coaches and mentors our leaders. I am grateful for everything this essential oil business has brought to our lives!

I hope you will enjoy all the positive experiences too when you both reap the rewards of your success. When that happens, I hope you can say that your crucial contribution helped in your success!

Practicing Self-Care

There is no excuse for not doing self-care. Doing self-care is a must. It is a disservice to yourself when you ignore self-care. Self-care revitalizes you. Self-care enables you to be a better person!

Self-care recaptures your lost or low energy. It takes away the stress you have accumulated in a week or so. Doing self-care makes you more creative. You smile and laugh more. It makes you a happy person. You make more friends. It improves your overall health. Self-care makes you a better person and a more compassionate human being. Strive to be a better *you* by doing self-care on a regular basis.

You do not have to spend a lot of money on self-care. Here are some suggested activities to break your daily work or life's routine.

- Learn and do ascension or meditation. Practice doing this the same time daily, which is better than practicing at random times.

- Have a manicure and a pedicure once or twice a month.

- Take a weekly bath or body soak.

- Soak your feet in warm water with essential oils. Do this weekly while watching a movie at home.

- Use your bio-mat or your own sauna, or use the sauna three or four times a week.

- Follow an exercise regimen on a daily basis. Alternately, go for a bike ride; swim; take a long hike; do some brisk walking; try some weight lifting; and explore other exercise as you desire.

- Find a break time daily or every hour. Do simple stretching once in a while.

- Buy yourself something inexpensive as a reward for any milestone you have accomplished, no matter how small it is.

- Cook a meal for yourself.

- Be present to enjoy moments of peace and freedom.

- Get up early and read a few pages daily from your chosen books as your daily inspiration.

- Once in a while, change your scenery. Go for a short drive to another city or town.

- Schedule a time for a cup of favorite cappuccino or warm tea.

- Just do nothing.

- Practice less multitasking.

- Practice a yoga style of your choice three or four times a week.

- Learn a new fun skill, like dancing, painting, knitting, simple cooking, acting, comedy skits, etc.

- Take time for slow contemplative morning coffee or warm tea while doing gratitude journaling.

- Diffuse your favorite essential oil while relaxing.

- Get body massages.

- Forgive others so you don't carry that burden.

- Attend live concerts to listen to live music of your choice or attend live plays.

- Arrange lunch or dinner dates with friends.

- Once a year, visit a place, a city, or a country where you have never been.

- Spend less time on the Internet or social media.

- Spend intimate time with your partner or spouse.

- Volunteer to any great cause you believe in.

- Attend a church service or a spiritual gathering.

CALL TO ACTION:

Write down self-care you are doing or are planning to implement:

_____

_____

_____

_____

_____

_____

_____

_____

_____

_____

_____

_____

Afterword

Life Is a Choice!

"IT IS IN YOUR MOMENTS OF DECISION THAT YOUR DESTINY IS SHAPED." –TONY ROBBINS

The direction of our lives is the effect of choices we made. We choose what we think and feel are right for us. Ability to choose is a matter of right and a privilege at the same time. At times, making a decision to choose what is right or what is wrong compels us to make a hasty decision. Sometimes, a hasty decision is a bad decision we regret later on.

If you find it hard to decide, philosopher Ruth Chang had this to say about easy versus hard choices.

> .... *Instead of looking for reasons out there, we should be looking for reasons in our*

heart… Far from being sources of agony
and dread, hard choices are precious
opportunities for us to celebrate what is
special about the human condition, that the
reasons that govern our choices as correct
or incorrect sometimes run out, and it is
here, in the space of hard choices, that we
have the power to create reasons for
ourselves to become the distinctive people
that we are. And that's why hard choices are
not a curse but a godsend.[9]

By now you know it was a pretty easy decision for
me to help my husband. To do so, I set aside
temporarily my other desire to become a life coach
and a speaker to empower women, but it is a
decision I have never regretted. There was no doubt

---

[9] Chang, Ruth. Transcript of her TEDSalon NY 2014 Speech, *How to make hard choices*, at 13:57.
http://www.ted.com/talks/ruth_chang_how_to_make_hard_choices/transcript?language=en

in my heart and in my mind that this business will work for the two of us.

Suffice to say, it's what is in our hearts that matter. So, after reading this book, what does your heart tell you? Will you give your spouse a chance on what she or he wants to accomplish, or not? Will you help her or him? Will you be there with your partner when it is time to celebrate all the success?

I know there are thousands of support spouses making a big difference in this business. You have the chance now not only to help your partner or spouse, but also—in doing so—to make a difference in the lives of other distributors and product consultants. This has been my path, and I've done it from my heart. Join me, and begin the amazing journey that comes with fully supporting your partner's future success!

Book Suggestions

Please visit www.crucialpartner.com for a list of suggested books and other reading materials.

Other books by Liz Wilder:

How Did You Do That! Kingsbury, Gail (Fall 2009), a best-selling book. This is a collaborative book by Mark Victor Hansen, Brendon Burchard, Liz Wilder and other folks just like *You* who went for *It and prospered!*
https://goo.gl/BOcijj

Realistic Outsourcing in the Philippines—How To Establish Successful Working Relationships with Filipinos. Wilder, Liz. (2011).
Do you want to improve your working relationships with your Filipino outsourcers or virtual assistants? This book will give you ideas on how to better connect with your virtual assistants, and gain higher work production output from them.
https://goo.gl/eM1P5v

About The Author

Liz Wilder is a best-selling author. She has been learning and practicing the multifaceted aspects of multilevel marketing since 2011. She has been an entrepreneur since she was in elementary school, as a fish vendor in Manila, Philippines. At that young age, she learned the value of courage and hard work: hard work develops self-worth. Self-worth leads to self-esteem. Courage and self-esteem lead to success.

After thirty-five years in the corporate environment, including private and government settings, Liz developed an open-minded attitude to embrace something new. Studying the MLM business and the activities that go with its implementation were fun challenges to her. Her positive mindset paved the way for the great things she learned about the MLM business. She believes it is one of the best and easiest ways to become successful as an entrepreneur.

Liz's formal degree is in social work and the legal field. She raised two children, now adults, on her own. Her experiences in surmounting and thriving on the challenges in life and in business qualify her as a great support in motivating and inspiring spouses to help make the business of the lead spouse successful!

Writing had never been in Liz's mind, nor had doing the MLM business, but look what she knows now!

"I want to help!" is one of her favorite expressions. Liz is also an aspiring life coach and a public speaker.

Do you need any help regarding how to become the crucial partner in your business? Liz can be reached at Crucialpartner@lizwilder.com